Picnic at the Seaside on Holiday

CHILDREN SAVING OUR PLANET SERIES

CAROL SUTTERS

AuthorHouse™ UK
1663 Liberty Drive
Bloomington, IN 47403 USA
www.authorhouse.co.uk
UK TFN: 0800 0148641 (Toll Free inside the UK)
UK Local: 02036 956322 (+44 20 3695 6322 from outside the UK)

Because of the dynamic nature of the Internet, any web addresses or links contained in this book may have changed since publication and may no longer be valid. The views expressed in this work are solely those of the author and do not necessarily reflect the views of the publisher, and the publisher hereby disclaims any responsibility for them.

Any people depicted in stock imagery provided by Getty Images are models, and such images are being used for illustrative purposes only. Certain stock imagery © Getty Images.

This book is printed on acid-free paper.

ISBN: 978-1-6655-8793-8 (sc)
978-1-6655-8794-5 (e)

Library of Congress Control Number: 2021907295

Print information available on the last page.

Published by AuthorHouse 04/15/2021

authorHOUSE®

Kate and Tom are on holiday with their grandparents and today they will walk along the beach and have a picnic lunch.

The sun is shining and Kate and Tom are very excited. They take their ball, bucket and spade.

There is a strong wind on the beach and the wind is blowing onto the land.

Kate's gran lays out a picnic for the children. They sit on the beach, drink water and eat their sandwiches, fruit and cake. As they eat and look around they notice that they are surrounded by empty bottles and waste plastic carrier bags that were washed up onto the sand.

Kate asks, "Why is all this rubbish washed up here on the sand from the sea?" Gran replies, "It has probably been blown onto the beach from the sea, but some of it may be here because people have dropped their litter here. They should have put it in the waste bins provided. That is very bad. Plastic carrier bags are so lightweight that they get blown about and carried by winds to distant woods and trees. Many finally end up being blown out to seas."

Gran continues, *"Plastic pollution is one of the greatest threats to the health of the oceans worldwide. It is known that plastic pollution affects sea turtles, seabirds, fish, coral reefs and many other marine species and habitats."*

"Yes," says Tom, "*We are meant to put waste in the bins.*"

"It's not just that," says gran. "The problem with plastic is that it does not break down completely naturally. It breaks down into smaller particles and eventually forms tiny fibre like particles call microfibre plastics, which get washed out to sea. In the sea it is harmful to the fish and other sea creatures which eat it. They do not realise it is plastic and not a food source. If sea creatures mistakenly eat plastic microfibres they can die. Plastics can destroy natural ecosystems."

"That's awful," says Kate. "What can we do to stop this?" Gran replies, "We need to reduce the amount of plastic we use and throw away because it is difficult to dispose of and it is damaging our seas and land."

"How can we do this?" questions Tom.

Gran replies, *"For example, at a picnic there are several ways to reduce plastic. We could use bottles which we do not discard after just a single use, especially those not made of plastic. We could use only reusable cutlery, cups and plates. We can sit on a straw beach mat, not a plastic one.*

It is also very important that we dispose of plastic bottles in the recycling bins at home so that the plastic can be properly treated and does not later harm sea creatures."

"*Plastic waste is a major problem. It can be burned, but this releases toxic gases from the plastic and carbon which pollute the air and can contribute to climate change. Some plastic waste gets buried in landfill dumps but it can take up to 450 years for bottles to decompose and up to 1000 years for other plastics to decompose. Plastic dumped in landfill releases toxins and causes air and water pollution.*"

"You will have seen," says gran, "That I wrapped your sandwiches in a paper bag for each of you. I did not use a plastic bag. In this way I reduced the use of two plastic sandwich bags, which would have added to the pollution of our planet."

Gran suggests that they play a game to collect plastic rubbish to see who can collect the most. Gran has three brown paper bags and the three of them spend some time walking around collecting plastic rubbish from the sand. They take the plastic rubbish back to the car to put it in the plastic recycling bin at their house.

Gran remarks, *"If all visitors collected a little plastic rubbish when they visited the coast, like us, there would be much less plastic microfibre waste in the seas harming our sea creatures."*

Used old fishing nets

She tells them, "*A business has started to re-use plastic fishing nets in Chile. Plastic fishing nets are often dumped into the sea and contribute to the plastic pollution in the oceans. The plastic nets are cut up and turned into recycled polyester and nylon pellets, which are sold to companies as a sustainable alternative for them to use as plastic. This is a clever way to recycle broken plastic fishing nets.*"

Tom and Kate decided they would tell their parents about the large amounts of plastic rubbish they found by the seaside. Also, how they picked up some of the rubbish for recycling.

What did we learn today? (tick the box if you understood and agree)

☐ We can use re-useable drinking bottles for water – not single use plastic bottles.

☐ We can use paper bags and not plastic bags for sandwiches.

☐ We can pick up plastic waste from the beach and throw it in recycling bins for plastic waste.

☐ Microfibre plastic waste in the seas causes fish and sea plants to die and this will damage our earth.

Find out what Kate and Tom had to say about the Great Barrier Reef in Book 10 The Oceans and Coral.

Children Saving our Planet Series

Books

1. **Tom and Kate Go to Westminster**

2. **Kate and Tom Learn About Fossil Fuels**

3. **Tom and Kate Chose Green Carbon**

4. **Tress and Deforestation**

5. **Our Neighbourhood Houses**

6. **Our Neighbourhood Roads**

7. **Shopping at the Farm Shop**

8. **Travelling to a Holiday by the Sea**

9. **Picnic at the Seaside on Holiday**

These series of simple books explain the landmark importance of Children's participation in the Extinction rebellion protest. Children actively want to encourage and support adults to urgently tackle both the Climate and the Biodiversity emergencies. The booklets enable children at an early age to understand some of the scientific principles that are affecting the destruction of the planet. If global political and economic systems fail to address the climate emergency, the responsibility will rest upon children to save the Planet for themselves.

This series is dedicated to

Theodore, Aria and Ophelia.

Printed in the United States
by Baker & Taylor Publisher Services